AF208370

NOT SO BORING

Activity Books Kids Age 6 | Vol -2 | How to Draw & Coloring

ActivityCrusades

Published by Speedy Publishing Canada Limited

HOW TO DRAW

CAN YOU COPY THIS?

Use the lines as your guide to draw the picture!

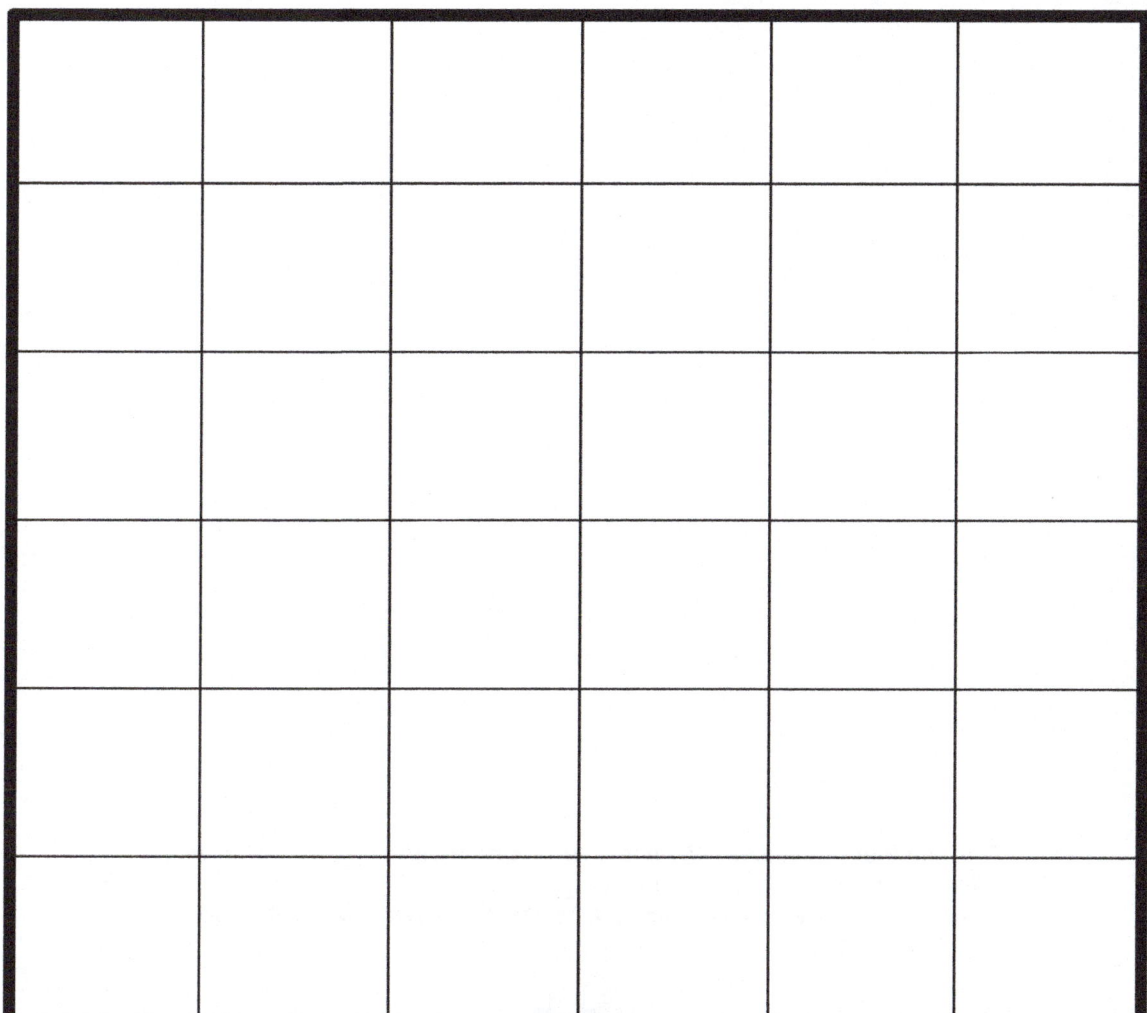

COLORING

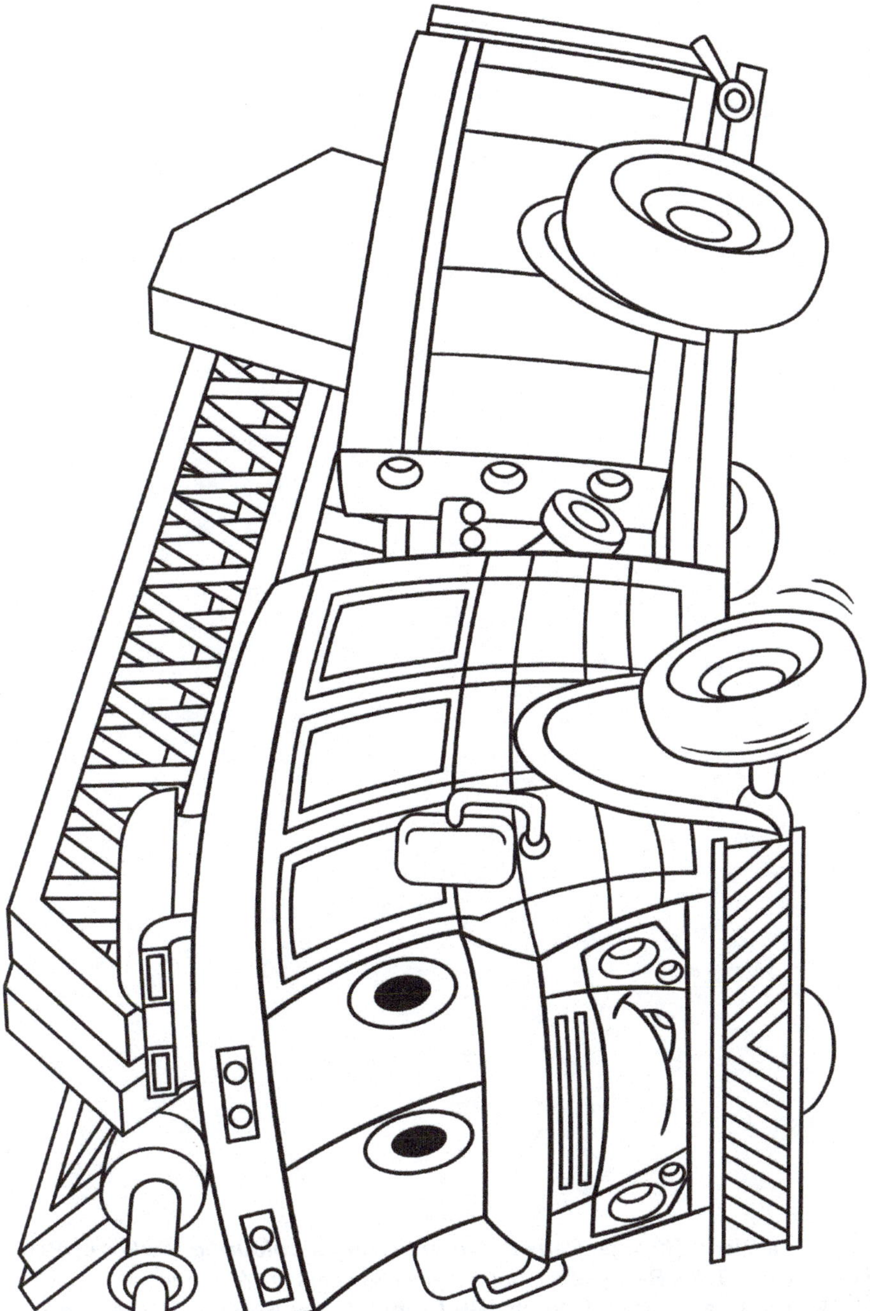

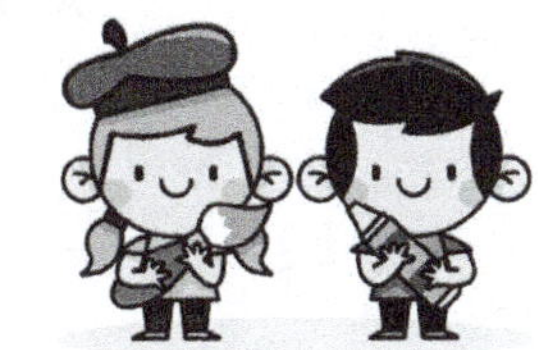

Made in the USA
Monee, IL
07 July 2026

56545677R00046